eurial Mission in a Church Café

Open Doors, Open Hands, Open Heart

Madeline Light

Vicar of St Stephen's Church, Norwich

Naomi Lawson Jacobs

Independent Research Consultant

GROVE BOOKS LIMITED

RIDLEY HALL RD CAMBRIDGE CB3 9HU

Contents

Church Mission Society supports the Grove Mission and Evangelism Series
At Church Mission Society, we believe that every Christian is called to join in God's mission, whether that means crossing the street or crossing continents, and we want to set people free to put that call into action.

Acknowledgments
The research for this booklet was generously funded by the HeartEdge network. We would like to thank the leadership team, congregation and café volunteers at St Stephen's Church, Norwich for sharing their time and stories in interviews and focus groups.

First Impression November 2023
ISSN 2399-6536
ISBN 978 1 78827 355 8

Open Doors: From Crisis to Community Café

1

The Chancel Wall Cracks

It was 8 May 2009, and a busy time at St Stephen's Church, Norwich. New incumbent, the Rev'd Madeline Light, was due to be installed later that day. From out in the kitchen, congregants heard a bang so loud they were sure it was an explosion.

There was a huge crack in the chancel wall.

A water main had burst near the church's medieval foundations. The fissure was a sign of extensive damage in the fourteenth- and sixteenth-century building. To allow for emergency building work, the congregation relocated to a borrowed church hall. They would not return to their own church building for three years.

It would have been easy to see this event as a disaster. Yet Madeline remembers the crack in the chancel wall as a blessing. God was giving an opportunity to this church at the heart of Norwich, with its often-closed doors and the threat of closure hanging over their heads. Could they respond to the crisis with grace and imagination, using their building to serve God and their community?

A Model for Entrepreneurial Mission

Fourteen years later, a redeveloped St Stephen's Church has become a hub for a mission of hospitality to the community, as the church engages with those around them in ways they could never have expected. The church café is at the heart of that mission, hosting and financing the church's outreach ministries. In an era when many people have no contact with church, the café encourages the people of Norwich to come through the glass doors, spend time with volunteers from congregation and community, and take part in the life of the church.

For many years, the church has felt a call to open their doors to lonely, elderly and disabled people. But the café has given the church the resources they need to serve and support local people from many more backgrounds: rough sleepers; prison leavers; people with mental health problems; book groups and remote workers. People from very different backgrounds are held together in one welcoming church space. The once-closed church doors are now open to the thousands who pass the building, every day of the week.

> As a small congregation, we would never be able to find enough volunteers to keep the church open seven days a week without the café. We would have closed doors again.
>
> Madeline Light, vicar

The café ministry at St Stephen's is a model of entrepreneurial mission that is distinctive to the church's own context, yet relevant to other churches. The church's city centre location offers unique opportunities for entrepreneurship. Not every church is blessed with such high footfall past their doors. But the church's *values* are key to the success of the entrepreneurial mission at St Stephen's. Their café ministry has been shaped by a vision for hospitality. They have sought to come alongside their community, sharing church life, resources and the gospel with them—a vision summed up in their mission statement: Open Doors, Open Hands, Open Heart.[1] There is no mention of commerce in that statement. And yet, although they have never set out to make money, their distinctive entrepreneurship has been successful, as we will see in chapter three. That success has enabled the church to do more in, and with, their community.

As we tell the story of St Stephen's Café, ask how your church's values can shape your own entrepreneurial outreach in your context.

Relational Gospel Hospitality

Christine D Pohl writes that the Christian church has inherited a rich tradition of hospitality, from an era when churches and religious communities followed the biblical command to welcome the stranger as Christ (Matt 25.35). As we receive others in God's name, we come to discover that we too are sojourners in a land that is not our home.[2] Today, many churches are rediscovering this gospel imperative to share hospitality as they share the gospel, through community-focused mission.[3]

At St Stephen's, Jesus is their model for community hospitality—Jesus who was both guest and host, and blurred the boundaries of these roles.[4] The church works from a *relational* model of outreach, believing that God's church should not stand apart from those around us.[5] The café allows the church to engage with, not just work for, the community.[6] It is the faith and witness of St Stephen's congregants in the café that makes this a mission of the church, as they share their church life and faith with their neighbours. St Stephen's Café is distinctly Christian mission, rooted in God's love for the poorest in our communities, seeking the transformation of society and the coming of God's kingdom.[7]

> We are actively seeking ways to invite community into the church. We want to be there, available, for everyone.
>
> Annette Uzoigwe, café assistant manager

What This Book is About

Throughout this booklet, we reflect on St Stephen's Café as a model for entrepreneurial, relational mission that is transferable to other churches and contexts.

In chapter two, as we consider how St Stephen's Café enables the church's mission of hospitality in their community, we ask how your own vision for community outreach could be furthered through entrepreneurial mission.

In chapter three, we explore the distinctively Christian financial model that has led to the café's success. We talk about how the church met challenges by bringing in paid staff, and show how volunteers—from church and community—are vital in their entrepreneurial model of mission. We consider theologies of commerce in churches, to prompt reflection on your own financial models.

In chapter four, we reflect on how entrepreneurial mission can create spaces where the sacred and the secular meet—amidst the modern perception of a gap between these domains—in churches that share God's love and presence with those around them. We reflect on the importance of collaboration and partnership, when churches cannot do everything alone, and ask how your church could benefit from partnerships in your community outreach.

> We knew there was no going back after the crack had to be repaired. But it meant that we could make it a community space—keep the medieval integrity, but make the building suitable for long-term use. And it's just gone from strength to strength. You walk in, and there's a real buzz. So many groups use the church.
>
> Margaret Gilbert, Café Friend and church member

2 Open Doors: Relational Hospitality and the Café Mission

St Stephen's has always had a call to hospitality.
Shona Jackson, former worship leader

'The church is the community chosen in order to invite others into it,' writes Ross Hastings.[8] Churches are not called to retreat from the world into closed buildings, but to seek the *shalom* that God desires for all—the peace and well-being of the whole community. This is the kind of hospitality that St Stephen's seeks to offer, as they '[nurture] a community life…into which outsiders want to come.' This chapter is about how their café has grown from a small coffee shop to a local hub, where St Stephen's shares church life and the gospel with those around them.

An Opportunity for Change at St Stephen's Church

In the years leading up to Madeline's arrival as vicar, the small congregation at St Stephen's had been threatened with closure more than once. The crack in the chancel wall was a catalyst for change. As work began to stabilize the building, the congregation began to ask what kind of church God was calling St Stephen's to be—in and with their community.

We were fighting for survival. But it was the challenge we needed.
Ian Murphy, long-term congregant and former organist

The modern-day café has its roots in a Saturday coffee service run by deaconess Pat Atkinson in the 1970s. Funded by a grant from Age UK, it brought lonely elderly people into the church. That small coffee shop would become the centre of a new vision for hospitality.

The café was important because it was the only time other than Sunday that the church was open, for two hours on a Saturday morning. And it began to grow.
David Daynes, churchwarden in the 1970s and today

Visibility and Presence

It began with a vision for glass doors.

The new Chapelfield shopping centre had recently opened near the church. In a count of footfall, more than 10,000 people passed St Stephen's Church on a single Saturday.[9] The church just had to make the most of that opportunity. 'We had a beautiful medieval grade one building in the centre of Norwich,' says curate the Rev'd Ian Fifield. 'It would have been appalling stewardship to have it open on a Sunday only.'

And so the church put hospitality and visibility at the heart of the building's reordering—starting with the oak west doors. These were replaced with glass, making it easier to see inside the church. It was their way of showing the community that they wanted the church to be open to them.

Trusting in the vision, the congregation gave very generously to fund building work. By 2012, a small coffee centre was open daily for two hours in the newly redeveloped building, keeping alive the original mission to reach local lonely and elderly people with simple hospitality. But this would be just the beginning of the café's story, and everything it has allowed the church to do locally.

The Café Manager's Story

When new café manager Beckie arrived in 2014, she saw the potential in the reordered, open church space. She imagined a café that would be a place of grace in the community, sharing God's love as it brought people into the church. With Beckie, the church committed to creating a café culture where those living in poverty could enjoy a coffee or a cake side-by-side with those with those who had more disposable income. 'We would have an older lady sat at one table, and a homeless man at another table, and they could have a conversation with one another,' Beckie remembers. 'It was beautiful.' To pay for this distinctive economic vision, Beckie instituted a 'guide price' policy, with no fixed prices for food or drink—just an offer for customers to pay more or less, as they chose.

> It was something that God put on my heart. I wanted to see the outworking of what grace could look like in a church café.
>
> Beckie Ward, café manager

A small team of coffee centre volunteers, who had long been committed to raising money for the church, were understandably nervous about the payment policy change. What if the rebranded St Stephen's Café could not cover its own costs?

They need never have worried. The Norwich community responded positively to a very different model of commerce in the city centre, as we will see in chapter three. As customers matched discounts with donations, the café team knew that God was honouring their vision of a café with a culture of grace.

Nine years after Beckie's arrival, the café remains financially sustainable. As they outgrew their domestic kitchen, their success encouraged them to install a commercial kitchen. It now allows them to serve more customers—171 people a day in 2022.[10]

The church's visibility continued to grow after further building work to transform the church space into a safe, accessible home for the café. As the community answered the invitation to come in, the church began to understand—and meet—the needs that local people brought through their open doors.

> Without the café, St Stephen's would have greatly struggled. Our presence, Monday to Saturday, is really important.
>
> Ian Fifield, curate

A Listening Ear: Church Presence Through Volunteering

As in every British city, loneliness is a growing problem in Norwich.[11] Clare Melia, St Stephen's community worker, remembers how the church began to meet that need through the café. 'We started to see the same faces—people who would come in every day, at the same time.' Friendship groups began to form around the large café tables. 'It was a safe, warm and friendly place for them…an alternative to isolation at home.'

In 2023, the church helps address loneliness through Café Friends—volunteers whose role is to engage with customers who would like to talk.

> People just want to be able to chat with someone. It's an important ministry. We forget how many lonely people there are. And sometimes we forget, to be honest, how much the church can offer to people.
>
> David Daynes, churchwarden

Café Friends spend their dedicated volunteer shifts not serving coffee, but being with people. 'Some people have just got a really natural way of chatting to anyone, encouraging them in their day and listening,' says café manager Beckie. Most of the Café Friends are church members. It makes for a strong link between the congregation and the café. Café Friends can offer prayer—gently, and without obligation—to any guest who would like it. And as members of the community begin to trust church members and volunteers, they sometimes open up about their deeper needs. David remembers a man experiencing depression who often came to the café; volunteers and church members offered him time and care. Anne spent time with a veteran from Northern Ireland dealing with difficult memories from military service, who just wanted someone to know he was struggling.

> Café Friends make links with people, and then people feel that they've got a link with the church. It's really valuable ministry.
>
> Margaret Gilbert, Café Friend and church member

'Hospitality…emerges from a willingness to create time and space for people,' writes Pohl.[12] In a society that often prioritizes busyness over relationship, sharing time can show we value those who enter our churches. Through a simple offer of time and space, the café provides a culturally appropriate way for the church to build relationships with older people, disabled people and those experiencing loneliness.

A Volunteer-run Café

Although the café team is managed by paid staff, most who serve there are volunteers. This is not merely a way to run a church café cheaply. The church's commitment to working with and supporting volunteers is the bedrock of their relational mission. 'It's a huge part of what makes this *Christian* entrepreneurship,' says Madeline.

Beckie and her assistant managers manage a team of between twenty and thirty volunteers. They embrace help from outside the church, which includes offering opportunities to people leaving prison and unemployed people, in a supported setting. It takes careful management to hold together such a diverse café team. 'We've got some volunteers from the church that love the church and want to share the gospel,' Beckie says. 'We've got some that are not Christians, but who like the way the church does things. We've got people with various disabilities and people with mental health struggles, who have found their safe place here.' Volunteering at the café is supported by policies and procedures, including policies on 'Acceptable and Unacceptable Behaviour' and 'Working with the Public,' which are signed and followed by volunteers. Prospective volunteers complete an application form and new volunteers take part in induction which includes risk assessments, GDPR and confidential declaration forms. Volunteers agree to biblically-based principles such as establishing good working relationships ('And let us consider how we may spur one another on toward love and good deeds' Hebrews 10.24). Together with contracts for paid staff, these volunteering agreements set out the conduct expected of all those who work in the church, whether Christians or not, so that all volunteers may flourish together in this Christian community.

Of course, the café could not function without volunteers. But volunteering is good for the community, too. 'The café offers more to the volunteers than it does for the customers,' Madeline says. Some volunteers join the church's mission because they are lonely. Others want to support the church's good work in the community. Working with volunteers is part of the church's mission to be with their community, sharing the presence of Jesus with them.

> A new volunteer started this year, who had low self-esteem. She hadn't found it easy to find employment. But now she's doing a [training] course.
>
> Beckie Ward, café manager

The Volunteer's Story

Over a decade, Frank's journey has taken him from café patron, to regular volunteer, to church member, as the church has met his simple need for human connection and friendship.

Frank first came to the café in distress. 'I was having mental health difficulties,' he remembers. 'I just wanted to talk to someone. And I was walking past the church, and I noticed a sign saying "Coffee shop open." I thought, maybe there'll be someone in there I can talk to.' Frank was greeted at the door by a volunteer from the church, who offered him the listening ear he needed. The café quickly became the one place Frank knew he could find support when he was lonely.

Noticing that Frank was becoming a regular, the café team suggested he volunteer. It was a chance for him to give back to the café community. 'I found I enjoyed serving and supporting other people,' Frank remembers. It was about a year later when he began to come to church services at St Stephen's. 'I gradually came to become a Christian,' he remembers. Frank would go on to become a committed member of the congregation, serving on the PCC and offering a café patron's perspective on the church's outreach.

> They prayed for me a lot [at the café]. That was positive. On one level, it was just very good to think that they cared about me enough to pray for me. But also I think the prayers had some effect.
>
> Frank, former café volunteer and church member

Madeline feels there is no other way that Frank could have come to faith. 'He needed space, and little acts of kindness that were appropriate to him.' In the café, church members were able to offer Frank that safe space, where they could share God's love and presence with him.

A Slow Food Culture

'Offering food and drink to one's guests is central to almost every act of hospitality,' Pohl writes. Amidst a fast-food culture, St Stephen's Café has a distinctive commitment to slow, wholesome food. Their simple menu includes home-baked sausage rolls and cakes, made by church members and volunteers, and soups made in the café kitchen. Past attempts to serve more substantial meals made things more difficult for volunteers. 'So we pared back our menu, which was a blessing,' Madeline remembers. The smaller menu now means they can focus on building relationships, in a slower-paced café, where local people are encouraged to stay as long as they like. Wireless internet is available in the café space for those who would like to use it, but it is not widely advertised, and customers must ask staff or volunteers for the password. The internet service uses standard filters to prevent abuse. Given the café's mission to open the church doors to the whole community, those customers who come to the space to work are not discouraged. Having internet available in the café has never interrupted conversation. The café holds together those who use the space for many different reasons, with some coming to work in a friendly, relaxed space, while others consciously come to seek conversation and companionship.

> I think people appreciate that the café is not like Starbucks. You don't have to worry if you want to spend a couple of hours with a pot of tea—that's absolutely fine.
>
> Ian Fifield, curate

'Hospitality is central to the gospel,' says the Rev'd Jonathan Price, team vicar at The Beacon in North Lynn, whose church has set up a café inspired by the model at St Stephen's. Jon sees an echo of the heavenly banquet in spaces like the café, where the community is invited to share food with the church. 'At one point we were strangers to God, and then he welcomes us in and embraces us and eats with us. In the centrality of food, of belonging, of sharing, there's a glimpse of an alternative vision.' Slow-food culture is at the centre of this church's relational hospitality, as they live out God's love and welcome for the stranger.

For theologian Thomas E Reynolds, hospitality involves 'a mixing between guest and host that undoes the distinction between outsider and insider,' as we point to 'the God of both who is discovered redemptively in the meeting.'[13] In church outreach, we sometimes think the church has everything to offer; we may see beneficiaries as little more than objects of charity. But in the stories of café volunteers at St Stephen's, we see how biblical hospitality can blur the lines between church and community. Guests take part in the life of the church through the café, often through volunteering; some begin to attend services. At St Stephen's, they have discovered grace when they act not just as benevolent hosts to those in need, but receive from them as *their* guests—as did Jesus.

As Madeline describes it, this is a ministry of presence.

> People come because the food is good, but they also come because they feel cared for. The café team take an interest in who they are. Other customers take an interest in who they are.
>
> Beckie Ward, café manager

Points for Reflection

Principle: Let Your Vision for Mission Shape Your Entrepreneurial Ministry

- What opportunities does your church have for entrepreneurial ministry?
- Whom do you want your entrepreneurial project to serve?
- How might you ensure that your values and mission continue to shape that enterprise?

3 Open Hands: A Distinctive Entrepreneurial Model

Churches with an entrepreneurial mission must be beacons of a different kind of economy, writes Andrew Hartropp. We are to live and trade according to God's values.[14] That includes stewarding and sharing the resources with which a church has been blessed, so that the whole community may flourish. This chapter is about the distinctive entrepreneurial model at St Stephen's, and how it has been the key to creating a safe, welcoming space for the whole community in the café.

A Forest Glade in an Urban Jungle: A Distinctly Different Economic Model

Surrounded by the shops of Norwich and the Chapelfield Mall, the church has always sought to be distinctly different from the commercialism around them. 'I sensed that we needed to be a forest glade in an urban jungle,' vicar Madeline remembers.

For the past decade, St Stephen's Café has been financially successful.[15] The church believes that this success is the result of its distinctive model of commerce. The café's finances are integrated with those of the PCC, as the vehicle for the church's charitable aims: to enable a living church to interact with those around them. Ten per cent of café surplus is returned to the church's giving fund—an important financial detail in maintaining the close relationship between church and café.[16]And they sell only food, drinks and books in the church building. At times, the café's financial structure has been costly for the church. But they have committed to an economic model shaped by the church's values and vision—to serve the community, rather than to make money. They prioritize people, not profits.

Although efficiency is valued at the café, it is not at the cost of relationships. They resist branding, letting their simplicity speak to their difference. From the large tables where people are encouraged to sit together, to their community-donated non-matching traditional tea sets, the café presents an alternative to anonymous coffee shop chains. The personal touch works for the local people who come back week after week.

The café's success puts it at the heart of St Stephen's mission. It provides financial funding for the employment of the church's outreach workers, and a welcoming environment for much of the church's activity and partnerships. And, vitally, the café opens the church building to the community.

> It is very different from a purely commercial café. It is a community.
> Frank, former café volunteer and church member

Challenges and Changes in the Café

As we discussed in chapter two, for many years the church has had a vision for a café that would be a community hub for everyone, where the church could hold together people from different backgrounds. At its best, this ideal has worked well. But maintaining a safe space for those who are different has not always been an easy task for the church.

Not long after the 'pay what you can' policy was instituted, the church began to see changes in café clientele. More customers were using the space every year, some solely attracted by the offer of free food. Groups of rough sleepers began to dominate the café, in a way that felt threatening to the lonely and older people who are important to the church's outreach. Money disappeared from the donations box; the church dealt with night-time break-ins. 'It was becoming unmanageable,' curate Ian remembers. 'We were dealing with very challenging people.' The café mission to hold together diverse groups of people was under threat.

> It's not very glossy, when you're really engaging with people. The gritty stuff you have to deal with, in order to make this a safe space for everyone, is something that needs to be worked through and tried out.
> Biddy Collyer, long-term congregant and former PCC member

A New Financial Policy: Eat, Drink, Share, Pay What is Fair

If the whole community was to feel safe in the café, the church had to reconsider what was important to them—in their outreach, and in their commercial model. How could their payment policy show God's love to the community, while still ensuring that the church held onto ownership of the café? They began to mobilize the café's success to serve those in need in more structured ways.

> Our intention has always been to hold different people together. We did not set out to feed the homeless. We do, but we feed them alongside other people.
> Madeline Light, vicar

The first step was to adjust their payment policy. In place of offering free food, the café introduced a minimum price of £1 for two items. Years before the concept of 'paying it forward' was popular, the church began encouraging their community to do just that. The café's new payment policy was called 'Eat, drink, share, pay what you know is fair.'

A new community worker, Clare Melia, would be vital to this attempt to reclaim the church's ownership of the space. Customers who could not afford £1 for food would need to make themselves known to Clare. She could provide not just subsidized food, but structured support.

> I think over time as you see people regularly, day in, day out, that was when there were more hidden needs that started to become known, because trust had been built.
>
> Clare Melia, community worker

The Community Worker's Story

Prior to joining St Stephen's as their administrator in 2016, Clare Melia had worked in a local organization for homeless people. She remembers realizing how many café customers had deeper needs that only became apparent as they built relationships with church members. But staff and volunteers had no structured way to help meet practical needs—yet. Clare found herself becoming the church's *ad hoc* community worker, making informal connections with people needing help with housing, addictions, debt and more. 'When a need arose, as individuals came into the café, I knew who to call or where to signpost them,' Clare says. A sustainable café meant that the church could fund a paid role for Clare.

> Our philosophy has always been to let people do what's on their heart.
>
> Madeline Light, vicar

Today, Clare's work allows the church to support many more of those on the edge of the Norwich community. Clare advocates for clients with statutory agencies and even in court, and she has helped many café patrons find long-term housing. And since 2021, Clare has been running the REST recovery house for people needing more intensive support with drug and alcohol addiction, in partnership with Christian organization Green Pastures.[17] Clare calls this *investing in people*—a long-term commitment to those on the edge of the community who engage with the church.

> We're committed to the long haul, with these people. It's all about relationship.
>
> Clare Melia, community worker

Paid Staff Enabling the Café to Do More

Taking on a select number of paid staff has been vital to the café's success. Supported by staff, the congregation have been able recommit themselves to a café run on principles of grace. Professional expertise offers the structure that the café needs, if it is to be a safe space for the whole community—in everything from running well-being groups to hosting a local chaplaincy for people leaving prison. And because the café is a project of the PCC, the church can impose an occupational requirement that paid staff should be Christians. It is one more way their financial model ensures the café is a mission of the church. They have learned that committed professionals who share the church's values can be a driving force for creative entrepreneurial ministry in a church.

Thanks to St Stephen's reputation for caring for those who come through their doors, the church no longer fears theft or damage in the churchyard from those on the edge of their community. They invite them in. When people arrive in need or distress, volunteers know where to refer them.

> The disadvantaged in the city do not want us to fail. They are our friends. Once they trust us, they have given us as much if not more than they have received.
>
> Madeline Light, vicar[18]

Even more radically, the church can invite those who used to cause problems to volunteer and share in their mission. Hartropp writes that principles of biblical economic justice include empowering those who are in need, by offering opportunities, for example.[19] In the café, Clare's clients serve others, working alongside other volunteers, who all have a place to develop skills and confidence.

> In its professionalism, [the café] is saying something about the people who are in this room, and how we value them. We think you're worth our time, worth putting effort into.
>
> Jonathan Price, team vicar, The Beacon, North Lynn

The Response to a Different Commercial Model

The local community has responded positively to the church's distinctive entrepreneurial model. They enjoy meeting in a café that, rather than making money for a business, funds outreach and community support. Local people participate in the church's mission, joining them as volunteers, baking cakes, offering donations and spending time in the café. 'People come here because we are serving the community,' Madeline says. 'They are proud of to be part of the work we do.'

> People really like supporting this work. They know that when they eat in the café, they're serving the wider community.
>
> Clare Melia, community worker

A fully commercial café, run in the church building at arms' length from church life, would be unlikely to attract the local support that St Stephen's Café does today. Hospitality and relationship are key to the café's success.

God's Economy: Theologies of Church Entrepreneurship

The financial model of the café makes it possible for the church to be a light in their community. Its success increases the visibility of the church and actively brings the community alongside them in mission. The church is inspired in this model by John McGinley's theology, who argues that the church of tomorrow will be entrepreneurial in its culture, following where the Spirit of God leads.[20]

Madeline wonders whether some churches resist commercial activity because they have misinterpreted the gospel story in which Jesus overturns the tables of the money-changers in the temple (Matt 21.12–13). Jesus is condemning economic exploitation, she says, not entrepreneurship itself. 'It's not the buying and selling that's an issue. It's the way in which the buying and selling happens.' That is why they have sought to place the church's Christian values at the centre of the café. They continue to ask how their financial models fit with the values of God's economy, and how these models can support their mission to hold the whole community together in hospitality.

Church-run businesses like St Stephen's Cafe can model entrepreneurship that shines a light in the commercial world around them. As Samuel Wells argues, running an ethical business can create opportunities for churches to model 'a healthy, sustainable, just, ecological organization…in its relations with God, one another, and the created world.'[21] Wells says that when strangers ask what the kingdom looks like, entrepreneurial churches are prepared to give an answer, as they point to an ethical church-run business and its integration with 'every aspect of the community's life together, and say, gently but truly: "It looks like this."'[22]

Churches need to embody an alternative market, one which isn't based on competition, but based on cooperation - inviting people to imagine how different this [community] can be.

Jonathan Price, team vicar, The Beacon, North Lynn

Points for Reflection

There are a range of models for church entrepreneurship. Samuel Wells discusses several in *A Future That's Bigger Than the Past.*

Principle: Be Clear About Your Entrepreneurial Model

- What financial models might sustain your mission to your own community?
- How will your model impact your vision for outreach?
- St Stephen's Café is run by the PCC. What charity structure would best reflect your mission and fulfil your charitable aims?
- What balance of paid staff and volunteer support makes sense in your church's context? How far should staff and volunteers share your church's vision and values?
- What existing expertise in your congregation could you draw on, for example, to help with employing staff?
- What challenges might your entrepreneurial model create? How will you regularly review the suitability of your model to address the challenges it may bring?

Open Heart: Bridging the Gap

4

A church that shares the presence of Jesus will be attractive to those who may never before have considered church a place for them, Hastings writes.[23] As we have seen, the entrepreneurial mission at St Stephen's is relational first. The church seeks to invest time and space in their community, sharing God's love with them. They believe the church is not just for themselves, but for the whole of Norwich. As we will see in this chapter, the gospel is at the centre of this mission. This chapter is about the ecclesiology of St Stephen's Café, and how the church lives out its mission there.

Kingdom Growth Through the Café

A different kind of church growth is happening at St Stephen's. In the café, people slowly encounter a space of prayer and love that *is* the church. Church members engage with those around them as people loved by Jesus—not just as potential new congregants. Through relationship, some come to services, but that is not the immediate aim. 'First and foremost, we want to be good witnesses for the gospel,' says vicar Madeline. 'If that leads people to join us, or other churches, fantastic.' In Janet Hodgson's terms, St Stephen's are seeking *kingdom* growth, more than growth in numbers on the electoral roll. Kingdom growth 'glorifies Christ, who is the Lord of the kingdom.'[24]

> We seek to be a kingdom presence for the people around us, without pressure to join us.
>
> Madeline, vicar

The café seeks to bridge the gap between the church and the world around it. For many unchurched people, there can be a psychological barrier to entering a church building. An open-door mission like St Stephen's Café can help people to cross the threshold for the first time. 'The lovely thing is that because we're very open, people just need to poke their head in,' café manager Beckie says. 'It's not as intimidating as walking into the building for the first time [on a Sunday]. Here, they're already used to the café.'

If people come into a church with a café, they're now in a sacred space. They're now in a church. Maybe that might enable them to take the next step and come to a service.

Ian Fifield, curate

Once people get past that initial barrier, some feel more comfortable to attend services. Mel Wheeler is manager at Community Chaplaincy Norfolk, a ministry for people leaving prison, based in the café. 'We've had several clients who've become regular or intermittent attenders on a Sunday at [St Stephen's] services,' Mel says. 'They know they're going to see two or three faces that they know from dropping in during the week.' Several tables are now left in their café positions on Sundays, so that patrons can try services in a familiar setting. Through small gestures like this, the church is consciously encouraging the slow progression some customers make from café to church.

For those who are not yet interested or ready to come to services, the café invites people into sacred space. Many customers say they feel a sense of peace in the church. 'It's a great testimony,' café manager Beckie says. 'God's presence here does fill this place.' As they offer sanctuary in a living church, St Stephen's is changing perceptions of churches and Christianity locally.[25]

[Customers] like this place because it's different from other places. There's peace, there's a sense of God's presence.

Annette Uzoigwe, café assistant manager

There are many stories of café customers who have become part of church life, from the edge of the community. One homeless man—we will call him Simon—found help and friendship at St Stephen's, initially through the community worker.[26] With her support, he found a permanent place to live, and went on to join an *Alpha* course at a church nearer to his home. While he was still sleeping rough, Simon would sometimes come to services at St Stephen's, receiving communion just as he was—the unexpected guest at the table.[27] 'Did he increase the numbers on our electoral roll? No,' Madeline reflects. 'But did we show him the love of Jesus so he could respond positively? I believe so.' This is the relational kingdom growth that this church is seeking.

'How can we increase the numbers?' is the wrong question. Actually, the question is, 'How can we improve our relationships with the community?' The rest will follow.

Biddy Collyer, long-term congregant

Prayer and Worship in the Café

> The café isn't just a commercial enterprise. Prayer is at the heart of everything the church does there.
>
> Shona Jackson, former worship leader

For Pohl, church hospitality must be rooted in 'faithful labour that is undergirded by prayer.'[28] And at St Stephen's, 'prayer is part of the DNA of the church,' as children and families' worker Lisa Fifield puts it. Prayer underpins the church's ministry and witness in the café.

The church has always approached strategic decisions about the café through prayer, since those early days when the church was still shaping a vision for hospitality in the community. 'There was a real sense of waiting on God,' remembers former curate the Rev'd Matthew Hutton. He believes the café's success has come through obedience to God, by centring prayer in everything they do. As they prayed over their community through prayer walks, the congregation also prayed over the church building and café space, asking God to transform difficult situations they were experiencing there. They would become God's instruments to do just that. Praying for the overgrown churchyard used by rough sleepers and prison leavers, it would not be long before they would hear a call to serve those communities through the café and community worker.

> I don't think you could have the café without prayer.
>
> Gail Halley, church member and prayer coordinator

Prayer and worship are everyday features of café life. Each morning, volunteers and early customers hear Zoom-enabled Morning Prayer broadcast in the café. 'We will pray with anyone in need who wants prayer,' Madeline says, 'without making any demands on them in return.' In just one example, Café Friend Sally Clarke remembers spending time recently with a young woman who shared that she had an eating disorder, who was grateful for an offer of prayer. Café Friends always ask if guests would like prayer, and they do not force the issue if not. But prayer is one of their most important ministries with those seeking hope in the café. At the same time, prayer helps to establish church ownership of the café, showing Norwich that the church is God's house, into which all are invited.

'We have experimented with many different types of music in the café,' Madeline says, 'including organ music, classical music and Taizé music. We have settled on modern Christian music, played softly on a loop.' Christian drama, too, brings worship and church life into the café. 'This Remembrance Saturday we had a short drama which included sections of Scripture,' Madeline says. 'It was very well received.' The performance went on in the background while people enjoyed their coffees, leaving it open to individuals as to how far they wished to engage with the drama.

In addition to music, the church makes information on Christian faith and prayer available in the café space. A loop of notices on the overhead screen always includes a verse from Scripture. Members of the congregation have often taken on the ministry of leaving out Christian poems and inspirational writings for customers to take. And a free booklet called 'Try Praying' is always available in the café.

Prayer also helps the church to hold together a diverse volunteering community, says Café Friend Margaret Gilbert. The whole café team prays together in the kitchen before they begin their busy day, asking God's blessing on those who come through the doors of the church. Church members and community volunteers alike take part in that daily prayer. And for the congregants who volunteer in the café, their service is prayerful worship—and makes the café a ministry of the church.

> Being alongside the other volunteers, and just getting alongside people, is part of my worship.
>
> Margaret Gilbert, Café Friend and church member

But prayer *in* the café is only half the story. The congregation also faithfully supports the café through prayer, as the focus of the church's outreach. 'The café is continually prayed over,' says curate Ian Fifield, who believes this reminds the congregation that the café is integral to St Stephen's and their outreach.

Partnerships in Service

Partnerships with local organizations are one more way that the café bridges the gap between the church and the Norwich community. As McGinley argues, partnerships can be life-giving for churches reaching out to those around them.[29] The café gives St Stephen's the space and resources to host and work with other Christian organizations making a difference in Norwich. It is another way they can offer expertise-led support to people in particular need, while building their reputation as a church that supports those on the edge.

> We set up the café to make community, and that has informed all our decisions. When we became commercially viable we invested surpluses in building more nuanced communities.
>
> Madeline Light, vicar

The Prison Leavers' Chaplaincy's Story

Community Chaplaincy Norfolk (CCN) is a Christian charity that supports people leaving prison in Norfolk.[30] CCN Manager Mel Wheeler has been based in the church café for four years. CCN works with clients and volunteers of all faiths and none, but they are run according to Christian values. That makes St Stephen's Café an ideal place to host their work.

CCN clients build skills and self-worth through volunteering at the café. It is a safe place for people leaving prison to begin serving others, Mel says. 'Some of them come into St Stephen's and they say, "I'd really like to do something. Could I help here?" One client, Jason finds that with too much time on his hands, he can be tempted to shoplift. The café gives him a way to stay busy while giving back to his community. It is a safe, supportive place for Jason to meet his CCN volunteer worker, too.

> When I've been [to the café], there's always someone there I can talk to, for support. Or you could end up giving support.
>
> Jason, CCN client

The open café gives clients a sense of normality and community that they have been missing in prison. Clients can drop in and talk to CCN staff and volunteers alongside a diverse community of café customers. 'It hasn't got a big sign above the door, saying "Ex-offenders' project,"' Mel says. 'That open access is a beautiful thing.' She believes that being part of the café community can show prison leavers an alternative to old patterns of addiction and offending, through relationships with people who show them God's love. 'Part of the difficulty of breaking the cycle of offending is not knowing anyone who isn't also involved in offending.' Some CCN clients have begun to attend church services. But this is a reciprocal partnership, and it has worked the other way, too. When people who have recently left prison have come to services at St Stephen's, congregants have been able to refer them to CCN. As Mel puts it, 'CCN feeds into the church and the church feeds into CCN.'

The café's customers and volunteers benefit from relationships with CCN clients, too. On any day of the week in the café, an elderly person might be served coffee by someone on day release from prison. They receive from each other. As Mel says, 'No matter what [prison leavers] may have done in their past, there are still people who are keen to walk alongside them and see them succeed.'

> I've got a good network of people around me now, like I've never had before.
>
> Jason, CCN client

The church also takes advantage of smaller opportunities to partner with Christian organizations, as together they reach the communities they are called to serve. St Stephen's runs one of Norwich's Hope into Action houses, sharing shelter and friendship with homeless people.[31] The church holds well-being and mental health support groups in the café, in partnership with Renew Well-being and Kintsugi Hope.[32] In the past few years, the church has developed a thriving children and family ministry that brings local families into the café; several have begun attending services.[33] At the other end of the age spectrum, Anna Chaplain Margaret is championing older people who cannot easily get to the church building. It is another way by which the church continues to reach out to their original clientele—elderly and lonely people.

> Churches are so often focused on younger people. It's easy for older people to be forgotten.
>
> Margaret, Anna Chaplain

Churches need to know they cannot do everything themselves. Partnerships with other organizations can give churches the means to empower those who have been marginalized, sharing resources and opportunities with them.[34] 'The New Testament offers wonderful examples of church partnerships,' writes Hartropp, who believes that partnerships can be a witness to Christians' unity and commitment to God's kingdom, especially in societies and churches divided between rich and poor.[35] In cooperation, churches and Christian organizations can do more in the community. 'And then the world looks on and says, "See how these Christians love one another,"' reflects former St Stephen's curate Matthew Hutton. 'That would be an extraordinary example of unity.'

Crossing the Church/Secular Divide

The gap between church and society is a modern phenomenon.[36] As Madeline argues, for medieval churches there was no divide between the secular world and the church, when Christian organizations ran businesses for community benefit. The mediaeval history of St Stephen's was part of their inspiration for putting the café at the centre of the church building, as they reordered the church building with the community in mind. Bringing the community through the church doors offers more opportunities to share the gospel, Madeline believes.

St Stephen's offers just one example of outreach that bridges the gap between the church and the community, by meeting social needs and building relationships locally. Christian social action is growing in the church, as we respond to a world of 'rising needs and declining resources.'[37] As it does at St Stephen's, this involves being with those around us. 'You cannot change people's lives for them,' writes Samuel Wells, 'but you can walk alongside them and give them trust, challenge, and encouragement while they find resources and strength to make those changes for themselves.'[38]

Not all churches would describe such social outreach as *evangelism*.[39] St Stephen's members themselves have sometimes wondered whether their proclamation evangelism should go further.[40] While *Alpha* courses, for example, have brought some to faith at the church, these courses have been more successful in building relationships—the church's strength.

> The reason for the café isn't to get people to church services. That's a balancing act, because of course we would love people to find a faith in God. But it's community-based evangelism.
>
> Ian Fifield, curate

Yet the café ministry at St Stephen's could be described as holistic and relational evangelism.[41] As theologian N T Wright puts it, this is gospel mission, by which we proclaim through our (church) lives that the kingdom is coming.[42] Research shows that, today, sudden conversions are rare; slow journeys towards a commitment to Christ are more common. The *presence* of the church in people's lives is vital for those on gradual faith journeys, 'so that people might have the chance to experience the love of God.'[43] This is where the relational evangelism at St Stephen's comes into its own, Madeline believes. 'Much of what the café does is to increase sympathy to Christianity,' she says, 'which *is* evangelism, but along a continuum between total unbelief and total commitment.' For many in the Norwich community, St Stephen's is *their* church—whether they eventually come to services, or simply engage with church life through the café.[44]

But St Stephen's has also experienced a growth in numbers at services on Sundays. This is often because of the café, too. New members appreciate that St Stephen's is not merely focused on running a congregation, but on serving those in the city around them. Madeline calls this 'reputational evangelism'—an impact of the presence of this church in their community.

'Conversion is an inner event that...must develop from within,' Henri Nouwen writes. 'We cannot force anyone to such a personal and intimate change of heart, but we can offer the space where such a change can take place.'[45] The café allows St Stephen's Church to offer that space for change, as they share the love and presence of Jesus with those around them. God does the rest, Madeline believes. 'It's easy to think that the church makes converts. But God is the one who draws people.' As St Stephen's has found, when mission is centred on welcoming the stranger, God may change not just the community that engages with the church, but the church, too.

> It's a responsibility—meeting people, talking to people...You've got to discern the right time and the right place for sharing the gospel.
>
> Anne Murphy, long-term congregant and former reader

A Café at the Heart of the Church, at the Heart of the Community

At St Stephen's, a vision for hospitality has led them to make the most of their location and church building. In response to a crisis, they placed the café at the heart of a reordered church. They welcomed redevelopment of the path that brings thousands of people past their door daily from the local shopping centre, shaping a building that invites the community into a living church. Their work with volunteers is a vital part of their relational ministry. They serve those on the edge in Norwich, holding them together in one church building, open to all.

For these reasons and more, a traditionally commercial model would never have fit the vision for relational gospel hospitality at St Stephen's. Your church might find that a different entrepreneurial model fits your own mission. But you may still find, with St Stephen's, that entrepreneurial mission is your vehicle to be 'the church at its best...bringing people together in a lonely and individualist society,' into a sacred space where relationship and service can flourish, and where church members can love our neighbours as ourselves.[46]

> We're using the church building, every day of the week. That's a declaration of our interpretation of faith: that belief and action are integral with each other.
>
> Madeline Light, vicar

Points for Reflection

Principle: Entrepreneurial Mission Can Bridge the Gap

- Where do you see gaps between your church and your community?
- How could entrepreneurial mission ease local people's first step into your church?
- Whom might you be called to work with, for the sake of the gospel?
- How will your mission and values determine that choice of possible partnerships?

Notes

1 https://www.ststephensnorwich.org/

2 C D Pohl, *Making Room: Recovering Hospitality as a Christian Tradition* (Grand Rapids, MI: Eerdmans, 1999).

3 *ibid*; H J M Nouwen, *Reaching Out: The Three Movements of the Spiritual Life* (Glasgow: William Collins, 1976).

4 Pohl, *Making Room, op cit.*

5 S Wells, *Incarnational Mission: Being with the World* (Norwich: Canterbury Press, 2018).

6 *ibid.*

7 S Wells, R Rook and D Barclay, *For Good: The Church and the Future of Welfare* (Norwich: Canterbury Press, 2017), p 36.

8 R Hastings, *Missional God, Missional Church: Hope for Re-evangelizing the West* (Downers Grove, IL: InterVarsity Press, 2012) p 130.

9 Number provided by Sally Clarke, church member, who undertook counts of foot-fall past the church from 9am till 5pm on two separate Saturdays.

10 Estimate based on hot-drinks sales.

11 Loneliness is a growing problem in Britain, where 3 million people say they sometimes or always feel lonely. Department for Culture, Media and Sport, *Community Life Survey 2021/22: Wellbeing and Loneliness.* Available at: https://www.gov.uk/government/statistics/community-life-survey-202122/community-life-survey-202122-wellbeing-and-loneliness

12 Pohl, *Making Room, op cit.*

13 T E Reynolds, *Vulnerable Communion: A Theology of Disability and Hospitality* (Grand Rapids, MI: Brazos Press, 2008) p 243.

14 A Hartropp, *God's Good Economy: Doing Economic Justice in Today's World* (London: InterVarsity Press, 2019).

15 In 2022, the first full operating year after COVID-19 measures ended, café takings were £152,000, representing sales of 51,000 hot and cold drinks and 43,000 food items. After paying for supplies and the salaries of café staff and several outreach staff, the café pays a tithe to the church's giving fund and contributes to the running costs of the church building.

16 The St Stephen's giving fund supports other Christian charities.

17 https://www.greenpastures.co.uk/about-us

18 M Light, *A Pattern of Grace* [unpublished].

19 Hartropp, *God's Good Economy, op cit.*

20 J McGinley, *The Church of Tomorrow: Being a Christ-centred People in a Changing World* (London: SPCK, 2023) p 152.

21 S Wells, *A Future That's Bigger Than the Past: Catalyzing Kingdom Communities* (Norwich: Canterbury Press, 2019) eBook ed.

22 *ibid.*

23 Hastings, *Missional God, Missional Church, op cit.*

24 J Hodgson, *Mission from Below: Growing a Kingdom Community* (Durham: Sacristy Press, 2019).

25 'Sanctuary' was one of several missional words used by the congregation to describe their early vision for a church offering hospitality in their community. B Collyer, *The Legacy of Richard Caister* (self-published, 2022).

26 'Simon' is a pseudonym. Some details of his story have been changed to maintain his anonymity.

27 Wells, *God's Companions, op cit.*

28 Pohl, *Making Room, op cit.*

29 McGinley, *Church of Tomorrow, op cit,* p 152.

30 https://norfolkchaplaincy.org.uk/

31 https://www.hopeintoaction.org.uk/

32 https://www.renewwellbeing.org.uk/; https://kintsugihope.com/

33 In one school term in 2022, children's outreach engaged with 66 families from the community.

34 Wells, *Incarnational Mission, op cit.*

35 Hartropp, *God's Good Economy, op cit.*

36 Citing Bretherton, Ross argues that the early church 'encompassed both personal/household and public/political spaces (*oikos* and *polis*),' and draws on Church of England reports calling the church back to that historical public role. C Ross, '"Often, Often, Often Goes the Christ in the Stranger's Guise": Hospitality as a Hallmark of Christian Ministry,' *International Bulletin of Missionary Research* 39, no 4 (2015), p 178; L Bretherton, *Christianity and Contemporary Politics: The Conditions and Possibilities of Faithful Witness* (Chichester: Wiley Blackwell, 2010) p 150.

37 Wells *et al, For Good, op cit,* p 22. Ninety per cent of churches were addressing at least one social issue in 2016; 10 million people in the UK engage with church-based community services. *For Good,* p 28.

38 Wells, *Incarnational Mission, op cit*, p 234.

39 S Kuhrt, *I Heard it Through the Grapevine: Developing a Social Mission Project Within the Local Church* (Grove Evangelism booklet Ev 105) p 10.

40 The team behind the *Alpha* course identify several models of evangelism in the New Testament. They argue that proclamation evangelism like *Alpha* should be one part of a wider programme of church evangelism that includes holistic or relational mission, which addresses social justice issues and builds relationships. James Heard, *Inside Alpha: Explorations in Evangelism* (Eugene, OR: Wipf and Stock Publishers, 2012) pp 30–31.

41 *ibid,* pp 30–31.

42 Kuhrt, *I Heard it Through the Grapevine, op cit,* p 10.

43 B Hewitt, *Faith Journeys: Summary of Research* (Kettering: 9Dot Research, 2018) p 7. Available online: https://d3hgrlq6yacptf.cloudfront.net/613f4f2fb49ba/content/pages/documents/faith-journeys-research-report-20th-november-2018-docx.pdf

44 Church of England research has found that congregations that experience growth tend to be incarnational and relational in their mission and outreach, as St Stephen's Café seeks to be. Church Commissioners for England, *From Anecdote to Evidence: Findings from the Church Growth Research Programme 2011–2013* (London: Church of England, 2014) p 20. Available online: https://www.churchofengland.org/sites/default/files/2019-06/from_anecdote_to_evidence_-_the_report.pdf

45 Nouwen, *Reaching Out, op cit,* p 75.

46 Ross, 'Often, Often,' *op cit*, p 178.